Going

poems by

Richard N. Matzen, Jr.

Finishing Line Press
Georgetown, Kentucky

Going

Copyright © 2017 by Richard N. Matzen, Jr.
ISBN 978-1-63534-109-6 First Edition
All rights reserved under International and Pan-American Copyright Conventions.
No part of this book may be reproduced in any manner whatsoever without written permission from the publisher, except in the case of brief quotations embodied in critical articles and reviews.

ACKNOWLEDGMENTS

With love to my parents, Richard and Alice Matzen.

Publisher: Leah Maines

Editor: Christen Kincaid

Cover Art: Richard N. Matzen, Jr. Photography

Author Photo: Danny Hart Photography

Cover Design: Elizabeth Maines

Printed in the USA on acid-free paper.
Order online: www.finishinglinepress.com
　　　　　also available on amazon.com

Author inquiries and mail orders:
Finishing Line Press
P. O. Box 1626
Georgetown, Kentucky 40324
U. S. A.

Table of Contents

Summer Starts

Early Summer 1
Tradition 2
Yuccas 2
Wabash Friday 3
LA Land 4
Prisoners 5
Twisted Ride 5
Hidden Rides 6
Descending 6
Jacaranda Trees 7
Going Away 7
Hansen Dam 8
Park the Commute 9

Mid-Summer Heat

A Park 11
A Nursery 12
Family Park 13
Bullhorn 14
Sunset Mercy 15
In Another State 16
Summer Heat 17
Going 17
Night Begins 18
Fishing LA 19
Dad 20
Fire 20

Summer Ends

Wilds 21
Sunset Left 22
Blues Stories 23
Fire in Newhall Pass 24
The Commute 25
Acting Out 26
Passing 27
Wanting a Place 28
Dust Storm 29
Willow 30
Fixated 31
Catch and Release 32
Recalling 33
Jump a Bit 34

Early Summer

Shift in between speeds again
commute fast-paced with piano playing,
another time streaming through my open car windows,
a jazz time passing through traffic while I'm driving away from LA.

Now near the coast
clouds drift in cool air
through the mountain pass—
soft gray lights,
a marine fog bank rolls
over the pass's highest ridges
slips over tan, cream, brown rock layers
consuming tilted color-coded strata
catching the last part of a sunrise leaving
as summer begins.

Tradition

The Subaru flies like a café
riding on playing soft jazz inside
and listening as I write on a writing pad
sitting on my knee, the other knee free to drive
to hold the steering wheel steadily.

Write the dusk down
with the interstate's pot holes and cracks
bending and beating tires
mixing with white and yellow road lines
drumming road noise, the road beats into jazz
a free mix filling in gaps in traditions and stories.

Yuccas

Watching the cars commute,
the first Yuccas bloom, tall stalks of white flowers
standing up to dot the dry river wash with white spots
among the sand and gravel beds
gray in the background.

Wabash Friday

An LA commute into a Friday traffic jam.
"Fuck it! Friday," I think and then read
"Wabash" written on the truck's mud flaps,
flapping in front of me talking about long ago—
camping beside its slow moving brown waters, quiet flow,
back in Indiana, a flow without brakes squealing
as the *Wabash* truck talks with big mud flaps
rumbling and whining "W-a-b-a-s-h."
Its motor growling deeply
dieseling uphill.

As stray teenage thoughts beat alive
in present time, I'm back in the old river's slow flow,
Wabash, with foam, and swirls, and froth fringing its banks,
the froth looking like dirty soap suds ring around a bath tube.

Mud-packed river islands building and protecting places,
not swept away by river waters catching and stacking
driftwood each winter and spring flood
collecting at each island's upstream end, the log jams,
protecting the river islands as the dirt flows and mounds
and builds ground under the islands,
even as the river cuts away more dirt,
pouring black into the muddy water
while some Maple trees holds back
the black dirt keeping it from all falling
into the muddy water flooding the Wabash.

Wabash truck cuts me off,
the 18-wheeler tearing up the upgrade,
pushing me aside like a tree trunk, not meant to float by,
pushing me into mud and gravel, a slight swirl and tire spin,
lost in an eddy by an island, floating and spitting gravel,
caught in still muddy water sliding by
from concrete barriers behind *Wabash* truck
mud flaps flapping, driving carelessly uphill.

LA Land

Light gray air masses slide in the morning wind
slipping in between mountains, turn to see layers
—foothills, mountains, rolling ridge lines, no central peaks—
an elevated horizon of mountains running east-to-west,
San Gabriel Mountains colliding into Santa Susana Mountains
breaking down in Newhall Pass amid steady crackling,
a prolonged hissing of pops and snaps: crackling electric lines.

I drive descending the road going into lower noises and lights
watching the overcast—fog and clouds hang while sunshine seeps in between—
the gray light and electric crackling continuously in high voltage
snapping, crackling, popping away, high strung overhead
like mini-firecrackers going off along the ten-story-tall steal towers
marching in lines carrying high tension—snapping, crackling, popping—
as the electric lines connect to the transformer station.

Below Newhall Pass, crisscrossing electric lines
converge and spread an electric life across LA's valleys
crackling, snapping, popping an electric life, the soul of a universe
coming from Bonneville Dam to LA proper.

Prisoners

LA County Sheriffs
driving the prisoner bus,
a shiny silvery bullet with black markings
and black trim outlining black-tinted windows
making no eye contact as it shoots by
with prisoners going down the interstate
going impenetrably deep into distances,
passing away prisoners down the interstate
gone from sight in the LA prisoner bus.

§

Twisted Ride

To my left on the horizon, a blue sky,
then red and orange tinted clouds hang in sunset
like California's blood red oranges' insides,
ruby-red fading into yellow into orange pulp fading into dark purple pulp
looking like a bruise, a hint of black, a little fungus or mold perhaps
growing on a side, a cloud's side in sunset
turning from yellow, red, orange
into black overtaking the sun.
The blood red orange drops out of sight.

On a California freeway zipping into a lane
beside Magic Mountain, an amusement park,
another exit taking drivers away,
taking me away while the traffic fills
with police going away
in a twisted drive
leaving others on a roller coaster.

Hidden Rides

On the interstate, secrets lie in neat rows of red taillights,
the artificial lights negating night's come-on
to the brown, mounded hills softly lit
with indirect darkness and sunset yellows,
soft among grays and other shades
of a real night's coming on in cool air
the breeze with the moon rising through the mountain pass,
cold-lunar-white crossing elevated concrete bridges
linking traffic lanes, interstates—5, 14, 210—
all the white and red lights car lights
lined up with yellow and white lines
dashing on the road,
hidden and opened in all the rides.

Descending

Hands curled through the steering wheel and BANG.
Bang a slow two-beat rhythm into a valley
curling around brown hills—driving/beating,
writing/watching—so many cops pulling an 18-wheeler over.
Even more patrol cars cruise by while I glide
and return to a valley with my Blues
beating another time.

Jacaranda Trees

Beside the interstate on the city street
grows the Jacaranda trees standing in full bloom,
equally spaced apart, equal in height lining the streets
displaying large public drooping combs of purple flowers.

Between Jacarandas, Crape Myrtles grow short,
each with its lavender, scarlet, or violet combs
of banana-shaped flowers dipping down,
radiating out subdued psychedelic colors
hung against dark green leaves,
hung over concrete gray
as people walk by.

Going Away

Crossing traffic at 5 PM
—writing, drumming, swinging jazz—
be-bopping a way downhill on a sunny day
digging a tranquil scene
in the thick of I-5 and 210 traffic.

Off work, my mind, a nervous drummer
pushing pedals, snapping feet,
controlling tempo—snare, bass, tom-tom drums…
cymbals, ride and hi-hat—a drum kit pushing time
forward like scat singing, going away too quickly
in the drive to create new rhythms and tunes.

Hansen Dam

Drive and breath LA's hazy air and car fumes
on the freeway gliding to Hansen Dam exit.
Commute in June gloom,
in an odd mixture of marine layers,
low lying clouds and fog banks.
Then in a break among low clouds,
the brown smog layer sits on the horizon
away from I-210.

Off the exit, Hansen Dam on the horizon,
a two-mile-long dike shaped like a crescent moon,
dropped on earth but built to stand as tall a ten-story building,
a long curved block, an earthen concrete snake like earlier ones
made by ancient Mound Builders in the Midwest, living earthworks.

In the distance, the two-mile-long dike
topped by five-stories of large rocks and boulders
securing the crest and below there,
the dirt, brushes and woods
and the swamps.

In the dam's middle,
a massive concrete face
with gaping holes at the bottom,
tubular holes like stuck open jaws
muzzled by car-sized grates.
Their silence keeps logs at bay
stuck in the grates.

Behind them down under,
gaping holes drain into concrete channels,
outside the dam to the other side,
channels that can take water down
to rectangular stair-stepped filtering ponds.
All dry now; the water long gone to LA.

In the dam's core,
above its massive concrete middle sits
the seven, quarter-mile wide windows of air—
windows cut into concrete giving monumental views
to the blue sky.
On top flows the paved roadway,
running along the dam's top carrying runners, walkers, and cyclists
escaping LA's life before returning to the dry LA valley
below the dam.

Park the Commute

New Ford Focus glides,
a ride promising quiet
with satellite radio off.
Windows up.
Door seals,
sealed tight.

Road noise lost in repetition,
a commute for years
driving a little angry
at the traffic.

Off the interstate,
transform into a new scene.
Park and see
in the rearview mirror
the young brown horse stands
before scratching its butt
on a Pepper tree.

Black-socked legs stiffen.
Young Brown stands waiting,
switching its tail looking
at an old pickup truck.
A Mexican man emerges
and brushes Young Brown's shoulders, flanks, legs.

Families park and unload.
More horses being saddled up,
ready to ride when Young Brown trots out
between the pickups and trailers,
trots in a short, tight circle
around the man holding
the long halter rope at the center
of Young Brown trotting
in many perfect circles.

Watching, I write Young Brown down
into the park as the jazz genius pianist,
McCoy Tyner plays a piano through satellite radio

Summer Starts

across time so hard the piano bounces with his force,
pounding down on keys, bouncing rhythm and thuds,
thuds now heard in the background as the radio host says,
McCoy first played piano at the neighbor's house,
the boy prodigy borrowing a piano
to play away from home
banging the new music.

30-minute not commuting
to hear McCoy and hard bop—
Bird, Dizzy, Bud—playing a voice apart.
Hearing their suspending time in notes,
as I watch Young Brown
carrying a rider into the park.

A Park

Hanson Dam, a dirt parking lot,
where a sedan driver slows down
to call her dog, commanding him
to chase her as she drives slowly
to tease him along
before driving away.
He chases and barks.
They pass the couple in the red truck,
rocking slowly in invisible love,
swaying the cab,
before a new truck
spins tires to throw
tight dust curls.
Spinning like a top.
Dirty dust clouds pass by.
White clouds return to the sky
and cast moving shadows
over horses with cowboys,
tilting their heads.
Cowboy hats against the wind,
as sun passes and she rides by—
bareback, horseback, no saddle needed,
dark flanks poised in shorts with white thighs
and a halter top taking another turn in the park.

A Nursery

Beside the interstate
under high tension lines,
a hillside holds a nursery
where Angelinos won't live
but plants thrive with water.
All shades of green—outdoor flowers,
plants and shrubs mixed in with palm and fruit trees—
lined up in neat rows, even the large cacti sit
in a line in wood planter boxes six feet across
waiting to be sold back to the Angelinos—
all electrified looking healthy inside.

Family Park

Parked watching sunrays creep
up San Gabriel Mountain sides
washing them in red and orange colors
while cowboys ride and greet their families
for a day in Hansen Dam Park.

Under big leaved trees
sitting on the grass,
strong hip-hop,
a new be-bop playing,
kids on a sunny LA day
sitting with headsets
shining new sexy in the park
while younger kids play
soccer and baseball games
in fields far away.

Beyond, in the horse pasture,
black birds dive-bomb a hawk
who spirals down in short dives.
Then in a long curve,
hawk glides inches over ground
and up into a willow tree
landing for safety in the park.

Across the parking lot
in black jeans and black tank-top
leaving her blue convertible
with the top down, she moves
—tall, long, black hair walking—
all golden-skinned into her friend's car.

Bullhorn

Cop and security cars enforcing
the park's sunset closure
driving slowly around with twirling
white and red lights, a bullhorn voice
announcing, "Move along! Go!"
Drives out of sight.
And turns into quick blackness,
a pitch darkness extending to the horizon
covering trees, picnic benches, fields
while a slight blue lingers
on the edge of a sky.

Sunset Mercy

On I-210 in the foothills
breathing a little smog
listening to "Mercy, Mercy, Mercy"
recalling back in the 70s, teen years
hearing Cannonball Adderley play
a joyous song, "Mercy, Mercy, Mercy."

Listen to the orange glow of his horned wisdom
as the sunset breaths the last big note,
"Mercy, Mercy, Mercy,"
 celebrating departure in jazz.

Sunset.
Hovering at eye level
above San Fernando Valley,
a rusty red smog pancake,
a burnt brown extending to the ocean
going over LA and up canyons extending
from the ocean until the mountains
stop air flow at the edge.

Traffic jam behind,
I drive down the crest line
through Newhall Pass speeding
down the curving interstate
in the sunset with "Mercy, Mercy, Mercy,"
celebrating going away from the LA.

In Another State

For days with closed eyes
dad lies on his death bed
drying up and light,
no muscle,
just flesh and bone:
an unrecognizable man,
my dad.

His raspy breathes strain
on oxygen in the faintest way,
his bald head misshaped and shrunken
into an oblong thinness
holding only hearing.
Stiff in the hospice bed
facing a window
and the summer night.

I'm the last family to see him
as he sheds a tear and lays still,
hearing family voices
talking over him quietly
unnoticed for a time
before he passes.

Summer Heat

Black sedan parks.
Shiny doors open.
A man gets out.
On the other side,
a shapely woman leaves
a tattoo above her crack
going up her bare back
to her buttoned-down
white shirt, midriff showing.
She's gone in the back seat.

Going

Late afternoon, the pale moon
rises over-sized hanging full
over super-charged electric lines.

The suspended tension lines strung up
between steel towers that value
being permanently high strung,
never knowing the need
to stop electricity.

Night Begins

She's all shiny in a small silver car
when we make eye contact for a moment
stopping in a traffic jam on the interstate
in a sea of red lights and slow uneven speeds.

Slow weaving of cars passing each other
as interstate vision emerges
on top of Newhall Pass
where she's gone downhill
just after sunset,
lost in a mountain shadow.

Satellite radio playing "California Dreamin,"
a song from long ago present in bones and dry hillsides
bathed in sentimental dreams of night beginning.

Fishing LA

A few cars park,
each under a shade tree
protection from the sun.

Drifting across, a radio sings,
"I'm goin' fishin' Babe,"
a Blues tune taking me back
35 years ago to a professor
about a bass.

In my old poem
the bass languishes lazily,
floating over seaweed undulating.
Translucent fins move
enough to stay still
in the clear pond water
near shore but a foot below
the surface bathing in the sunlight.
He barely moves his large gills.

A few feet from the pond's edge
as my free foot taps floorboards
steadily keeping time
while my working foot puts
steady pressure on the gas peddle
following the interstate
as a bass moves in time.

Dad

In the end, starved to death, shriveled, suffocated—
withering in a dried skeleton of interwoven maladies
like earth letting go dried up in too much sun
dropping into a river, a dirt clod
loosened from the river bank
"blobs" before dissolving away
in river flow.

His last moments taken.
No water taken.
No breath taken,
letting go.
No heroic measures.
Dad's heart and lungs
fail like a mind loses
a last breath knowing
hearing is the last thing to go
before the stillness sets in.

Fire

Down the interstate,
burning forest and grass smoke
billows and rolls in waves
crossing roads and crackling
in brown heat waves
over drivers.

Wilds

Behind Hansen Dam,
a small artificial lake crowns a plateau
with a long blue corkscrew-shaped waterslide
touching its surface, touching a public swimming area
beside the roped off wild areas, marked off for public fishing
where an old men sits with buckets and poles dangling free.
Slack lines.

At an edge
in Hansen Dam Recreational Area,
the homeless camp on the lawn,
roll out blankets under tall pine trees.
Mostly men, a few women, homeless
among grocery carts, bags and boxes.

In the distance,
the two-mile-long dam
where many feet go along this LA edge
where tamale and taco trucks are parked
at one end and bell-ringing venders are ready
to sell walkers, riders, runners, bikers—
a way to quench thirst before going home.

Sunset Left

I drive with Caribbean jazz
a waltz swing beat, three-quarter time,
hearing it under the overarching concrete bridge.
Overhead, I-118 fast pulses veins and arteries,
pushes commuters by exits at mountains' feet,
pushes us under caged-in walkers and a man
standing in the middle of the pedestrian bridge
arching over the interstate, I-210.

West to connect Santa Susana
and San Gabriel Mountain Ranges
six concrete interstate bridges sculpting space.
Newhall mountain pass structuring traffic in my life
with single-mindedness, not to touch for safety's sake
while the sunset hangs
on my left elbow
while driving.

Blues Stories

Mountain skies and strong winds flow
through my car's open windows.
Stream air into backseats
where hard Blues plays
and blows back
up front to those sitting,
blowing a Blues,
a moan and groan
and shouting their stories
on the road filled with stories
going on without ending,
caught by the air on the interstate.

Fire in Newhall Pass

Interstate traffic flows and follows
curved and crocked lines going home
giving me time to write on a tablet
that sits on my knee like a banjo resting,
waiting to be picked and sung to with lyrics.

Open windows,
hear traffic making poetry
down into the road noise
—tire hums, horn blasts, crescendos—
voicing accelerating motors
vibrating high-pitched metal,
deep-throated cylinders and pistols.

Rattling engines roar
smell of burning grease
as diesel fumes suck up the interstate
keeping me in sync with my driving.

Then an erratic driver
drives slowly weaving in
and out of blocked lanes
while I creep forward
driving by ambulances and sheriffs
stopped at the blockage,
a wreck and dead body
beside the road.

Off my rear bumper,
she slips by too close
animated for a moment
shaking her long blonde hair
rhythmically nodding,
head bobbing
to the traffic.

Emergency sirens, moving rhythms
then lost in the wind's rolling red
brown smoke across lanes
forming low hanging ash clouds
as another message drifts into writing.

The Commute

The sunset casts orange light
on oak trees and scrub brush
descending down into the drop-offs
beside the interstate where I cling
to tilted mountainsides to commute
home on I-5.

Acting Out

Leave the park at sunset,
look both ways to pull out
into the far lane,
stepping on the gas,
accelerating down the road
to stop under the overpass
at a light.

A motorcycle cop stops too
in the lane beside me.
His finger gestures telling me
roll down the window.
His loud talk
gathers momentum—
sunglasses peeled off,
his chin strap swaying.
His eyes drilling contact.
Charging me with vehicular homicide,
he says, a real possibility,
the way I drive.

My illegally pulling out
into the first lane,
he says could kill him.
He shouts it's illegal
but no ticket this time.
He has no time to write.
Chin strap up,
he reeves his engine
and the motorcycle is off.

I drive back
onto the interstate going
in the opposite direction
when I see an old 57 Chevy *Belair* convertible
painted aqua and silver, a two-toner
driven by two 50-year-old guys
wearing high school letter-jackets,
dark shades, slicked-back hair
being Hollywood, being California
in the late 50s, early 60s, I think,
Howl out in '56, *On the Road* '57.
Piled into two characters—slick and carefree—
with the top down rolling along at 80 mph
on a southern California afternoon, 2010.

Passing

Old school,
driving with the stick-shift car
racing in the commute
driving by Lake View Terrace Exit
with eyes on the road
along with all those other
sunglass-tinted eyes facing west.

Facing the sunset
on I-210 coming
going under the I-118,
going by MacClay Exit
as the old car's throttle zips
up the upgrade listening
to Billie Holliday,
a sorrowful lilt
with my head
in the sun visor's shadow.

Wanting a Place

Mom's death means driving
in the early morning
in pitch black at 4 AM
alone with heavy traffic
on I-405 driving
to LAX to fly back
to my mom's Midwest home
to her inurnment there.

I'll see her cremated ashes
inurned into a mausoleum wall,
while I hope she has another place
to be among others and interacting.
A place, not a hole in the wall.

Dust Storm

My new car's
back in my hands
bringing me back into satellite radio
playing jazz and Blues again in the sunset.

In the rearview mirror, the brown wind
dense packs and stacks air into a dust
rolling uphill, a brown-out blowing over the traffic
cutting the sun-drenched slopes into brown foggy pieces,
into glimpses of ridgelines with a piece of blue sky.

In the dust storm hearing
ripping jazz rhythms
Max Roach tinkering
cymbal melodies
tom-tom, snare drum beneath
the bass beats his orchestrating
the coming percussive storm.

Willow

Hansen Park at night,
way off parked in the dirt lot,
an empty place near an interstate.
Step out into the full moonlight,
see a low hanging tree branch,
out of the corner of my eye,
a thick Willow branch
shaggy barked and close by,
extending my peripheral vision,
an extra arm reaching and blending
my eyesight like a wire being twisted
by the Willow tree, me being together
with the Willow branch out of my head
in a vision of night coolness smelling the wet grass,
seeing the baseball diamonds' wet dark spots,
breathing in the dirt smell
cool moist night air,
the Willow in me.

Fixated

Sitting on the interstate,
all the drivers look up
fixated on the helicopters
hovering overhead.
They're watching
a death on the interstate.

The crime plays out.
Hearing copter blades
thudding and churning up the air
loud as sheriff, ambulance, fire truck,
highway patrol cars fill the shoulder
in convoy looking for the upside down car,
a broken barrier and jack-knifed big rig.
A slow drive by and then I'm gone.

Catch and Release

Who fishes a soul out of a bucket of souls
puts one down with its little history
on the ground in another body
for safekeeping?

Recalling

Days after cremation
hours after her inurnment
parts of mom travel in her ashes
tucked away on the back seat
strapped in with a seat belt.
There in her blue urn,
printed with gold lines looking
like vines and butterflies
and floral patterns around her ashes.

A morning drive
under a Midwestern gray sky
in warm summer drizzle that drifts
in between fog banks and white mist—
vaporous strands of white mist
stand up weakly on the road
reaching up toward the sun
and gone in the rain.

Hailstones pound,
beating down knocks
on the rental car's roof.
The downpour thickens.
Hail rolls the roof like a drum,
no driver can see.

I pull over under a Sycamore tree
for protection as the car sways
rocking in the wind and rain
with mom behind me.

Jump a Bit

At the park as summer ends
with ice cream truck's tinkering music
high-pitched calliope songs
taken from the carousal
once at a fair playing over-and-over
rolling by slowly, tinny music
giving kids time to hear
they're going to get
more ice cream.

In the parking lot,
a parent and teen drive slowly
to practice teenage driving
gripping the wheel
and driving in circles
around outdoor light poles,
parked cars, horses, and more kids.

Parked, I hear the musicians play Mariachi music.
The dark haired, mustached man, bandolier
sitting on the edge of his Ford's tailgate crooning
with the new bass guitarist, heavyset white dude
shirt-tails hanging out to practice
harmonizing in time and place.

Across the park, she approaches
arrives at my window to tell me about god.
Lord no, I think and say, "Not today."
She goes away.

Happy hearing music, reading notes,
when a dark unshaven man stares
parked beside me and asks,
"Do you watch movies?"
"Yes," I say, too late to ignore him.

To catch my eye,
he drives his Jeep around
to park in the space beside me

and ask like a devil,
"Do you like really hot movies?"

I drive away, commute I-210,
and see my family's name
lettered on a semi-truck side
in big letters when I jump a bit
at the car that honks behind me.
But it's not there. The horn's on the radio,
squawking alto saxophone sounding off to trick me
as the sun goes down as I drive,
miss a heartbeat and go quietly
into the traffic.

After growing up in Bluffton, Indiana, **Richard Matzen**—inspired by artists and jazz musicians— published poems, poetry books, and jazz articles in the Pacific Northwest during the 1980s. Then, in order to pay the bills, he earned academic degrees and fostered teaching success. Eventually, his expertise in writing and teaching meant he created a writing center and writing department at Woodbury University in Burbank, California. At the same time, but after 30 years, his desire to write poetry rekindled itself to the point that in 2009, he began writing *Going*, a chapbook that he completed in 2014. Now, *Going*'s narrator, though images and commuting, tells a story about Los Angeles and the tensions between the need to stay in one place and never being totally in one place.

www.ingramcontent.com/pod-product-compliance
Lightning Source LLC
LaVergne TN
LVHW041555070426
835507LV00011B/1087